Interim report of the Commission to the European Parliament, the Council, the Economic and Social Committee and the Committee of the Regions on the implementation of the medium-term Community action programme on equal opportunities for men and women (1996 to 2000)

Employment & social affairs

Equality between women and men

European Commission
Directorate-General for Employment, Industrial Relations
and Social Affairs
Unit V/D.5

Manuscript completed in 1999

Document drawn up on the basis of COM(98) 770 final.

DBN: 1578956

ZZ
EM 242
99 I 56

A great deal of additional information on the European Union is available on the Internet.
It can be accessed through the Europa server (http://europa.eu.int).

Cataloguing data can be found at the end of this publication.

Luxembourg: Office for Official Publications of the European Communities, 1999

ISBN 92-828-6999-7

Printed in Belgium

PRINTED ON WHITE CHLORINE-FREE PAPER

FOREWORD

This is the Interim report of the European Commission on the implementation of the medium-term Community action Programme on equal opportunities for women and men (1996 to 2000) which was adopted by the Council on 22 December 1995.

The content of this report gives an overview of what has been done during the first half of the Programme. The basic features of the Programme and the ways in which it is organised and managed, are described. The activities of the Programme in relation to the six policy aims outlined in the Council Decision - achieving gender mainstreaming, mobilising all actors to achieve equality, promoting equality in a changing economy, reconciling work and family life, promoting a gender balance in decision-making and creating optimum conditions for the exercise of equality rights - are set out. After only two and a half years of project activity, specific research and networking the results are considerable.

The Community has been a driving force in improving the status of women in European society for the last 20 years. The first three medium-term Community action programmes on equal opportunities for women and men (1982 to 1985, 1986 to 1990, 1991 to 1995) have played an important role in improving the situation of women and in promoting co-operation at all levels. The current Programme was designed to build on the experience of these preceding Programmes and to react to new ideas, demands and challenges.

During the time covered by the report, important developments have taken place at European level; - the new Amsterdam Treaty, the placing of equal opportunities at the heart of the new employment strategy or the on-going progress on mainstreaming. The Programme, in spite of its limited resources, has contributed to these developments and shown the potential created by them and I am confident that this potential will be fully realized by the end of the Programme, to the benefit of equality between women and men in Europe.

Pádraig Flynn

TABLE OF CONTENTS

EXECUTIVE SUMMARY

The medium-term Community action Programme on equal opportunities for women and men (1996-2000) was adopted by Council on December 1995. It was designed to build on the experience of the preceding Community Programmes on equal opportunities aiming not just to consolidate previous activities but also to react to new ideas, demands and challenges. Many of these challenges had been articulated at the Fourth United Nations World Conference at Beijing in September 1995.

This interim report fulfils the Commission obligation, as laid down in the Council Decision, to present a mid-term review on the implementation of the Programme. The Decision sets out the six policy aims of the Programme (achieving gender mainstreaming, mobilising all actors to achieve equality, promoting equality in a changing economy, reconciling work and family life, promoting a gender balance in decision-making and creating optimum conditions for the exercise of equality rights) and describes the type of Community actions and supporting mechanisms to achieve those aims.

The content of this report has the following structure: section I describes the basic features of the Programme and the ways in which it is organised and managed, section II.1 presents the findings of the Programme in relation to the six policy aims outlined in the Decision and section II.2 illustrates the relevance and contribution of the Programme to developments and policies at Community level.

Alongside the six policy aims, are the strategies tested in the course of the Programme's implementation. These are innovation, partnership and transfer of good practice. These strategies have become a necessity for effective action contributing to the successful achievement of the policy aims and a gain in terms of organisational learning for the project working teams.

Gender Mainstreaming is the overriding principle of the Programme. It represents both a policy goal in itself as well as a strategy for achieving change in all other targeted policy. It is proving to be a complex, long-term approach. However, it is precisely this complexity and this long term perspective that make the activities of the Programme in this respect of such importance. These activities have included exchanges of experience, development of practical tools and frameworks for implementation and monitoring in various policy areas.

Indeed, the importance of the gender mainstreaming approach has since been confirmed in the European employment strategy and by the declaration of the European Council in Cardiff, in June 1998. The emphasis placed on mainstreaming by the employment guidelines and by the Heads of State and Governments at Cardiff was in no small measure helped by the evidence collected through different projects and studies funded by the Programme as well as by the work accomplished by the two expert groups of the Programme.

Another important underlying thrust of the programme has been the emphasis on ensuring complementarity between the Programme and the national actions or plans on equal opportunities. This has been done in co-operation with the Management Committee, which is made up of representatives of the Member State equal opportunities authorities. Thanks to this co-operation, a positive synergy has been created between the Programme and Member States equality bodies. In addition, the successful co-operation of the Programme with the successive Council Presidencies and the celebration of important Presidential events with the Programme's assistance and support give testimony of this vital co-operation.

The potential contribution to actual change at operational level in local, national or European situations represents the added value of the Programme. This 'built-in' added value is shown in the projects' results and will be increasingly achieved as projects embark upon the dissemination stage of their actions.

Another important aspect of the Programme's added value is the development of a common framework for co-ordinated actions at European level. Important concepts, such as 'gender mainstreaming', 'gender balance in decision-making' are now being developed in a European setting and are more and more linked with European policies, due to the platform for analysis and discussion offered by the Programme. At the same time the Programme is creating a common agenda for gender equality in Europe. This emerging convergence between the Member States is among the most positive side effects of the activities undertaken within the Programme.

I OVERVIEW OF THE PROGRAMME

I.1 Aims and Objectives

The medium-term Community action programme on equal opportunities for women and men (1996-2000)[1] was adopted by Council Decision[2]. It was designed to build on the achievement of the first three Community action programmes on equal opportunities for women and men. These previous programmes had played an important role *not only* in improving the situation of women in the labour market and in society *but also* in promoting co-operation at all levels in the area of equal opportunities.

The most innovative feature of the Programme with respect to the previous ones is the introduction of the concept of mainstreaming both as a guiding principle and as an objective, as set out in Article 2 and 3 of the Decision. The Programme will thus provide a reference framework to stimulate interaction and partnership in all domains and at all levels, whether Community, national, regional or local , with the aim of integrating equal opportunities in all Community and Member State policies and activities.

In order to achieve the specific aims set out in Article 3 of the Council Decision (such as mainstreaming, mobilisation of all actors, equal opportunities in a changing economy, reconciliation of working and family life, gender balance in decision making and exercising equality rights), the Programme (as per Article 4) disposes of the following instruments:

- Support to projects aimed at exchanging information and experience on good practice.
- Conduct of research studies in the field and monitoring of relevant policies.
- Dissemination of results of the initiatives embarked upon and of any other relevant information.

As set out in Article 5 of the Decision, the Commission and the Member States should ensure consistency and complementary between the activities undertaken under the Programme and under other Community policies or activities, including those relating to Structural Funds, education and vocational training, and those pursued by the Member States.

In Article 12, the Decision obliges the Commission to submit an interim report on the implementation of the Programme to the European Parliament, the Council, the Social and Economic Committee and the Committee of the Regions, by 31 December 1998. The present report fulfils that obligation. The report covers the first half life of the Programme period 1996 until July 1998. The Commission services are preparing an open call for tender for the external evaluations foreseen by Article 11 of the Decision. These evaluations which will be launched in the beginning of 1999, will help the Commission in the establishment of the final report due by 31 December 2001.

I.2   The Financial Framework

The total budget allocated to the Programme amounted in 1996 to 9.000.000 ECU of which 8.970.604,02 ECU were committed and in 1997 to 8.250.000 ECU of which 8.089.835,95 ECU were committed.

During the two first years of implementation, the Programme's appropriations were shared between the three strands referred to in Article 4 of the Council Decision. An amount of 11.798.254,56 ECU was committed to allow for the exchange of information and experience on good practice and as support for projects identifying and developing good practice and transferring information and experience thereon. Commitments for projects, seminars etc. amounted to 5.780.815,86 ECU in 1996 and to 6.017.438,70 ECU in 1997.

Financial commitments, totalling of 2.464.924, 25 ECU, have been made by the Programme in these two years towards activities observing and monitoring relevant policies and conducting research, including 17 studies, and towards the running of the group of experts on legal issues and the group of experts on "gender and employment".

The Programme has invested in rapid dissemination of the results of the initiatives embarked upon and any other relevant information for a total of 2.797.261,16 ECU, including the publication of periodicals, thematic publications and the Annual Report on Equal Opportunities. Of this last figure, an amount of 1.759.774,16 ECU was committed in 1996 and in 1997 an amount of 1.037.487,-- ECU.

PROGRAMME ACTIVITIES	1996	1997	TOTAL
Exchange of experience (Projects, Seminars, etc)	5.780.815,86	6.017.438,70	11.798.254,56
Studies and monitoring	1.430.014,--	1.034.910,25	2.464.924,25
Dissemination of results, information activities	1.759.774,16	1.037.487,--	2.797.261,16
TOTAL	8.970.604,02	8.089.835,95	17.060.439,97

The financial support granted by the Programme amounts to up to 60% of the total cost of the project according to article 8 of the Council Decision, the financing of the remaining 40% is to be provided by the promoter as own co-financing. Securing this 40% of the project overall cost has proved to be a difficult task for many project's applicants.

The reasons are, to some extent, inherent in the very basis of the Programme in that it focuses on the exchange of experience at transnational level and is not expected to fund local, regional or national action. However, the co-financing most likely to be found by applicants is linked to local, regional or national activities rather than to the exchange component itself. In the case of small organisations, there is an additional difficulty, in that, very often, the only contribution such organisations can offer as own co-financing is an in kind contribution –the work of their members.

The above circumstances have meant obstacles for a smooth financial running of projects during the period covered by this report and will presumably continue in the second half of the Programme unless further possibilities of co-financing transnational exchange can be more easily found in the Member States.

I.3   The Management of the Programme

For the implementation of the Programme, the Commission is assisted by a committee made up of representatives of the Member States. This Management Committee, as foreseen in Article 9 of the Council Decision, adopts the annual work programme, the general guidelines for the support to be supplied by the Community and the procedures for the selection of projects ; it also ensures the follow-up and dissemination of the actions supported by the Community, at Member State level. Given that the Management Committee is made up of representatives from the national authorities, it has played a major role in the development of the Programme in the Member States and further in strengthening the co-operation and exchange of information and best practice among the different Member State national authorities.

In previous Community Programmes on equal opportunities the Commission has been assisted by different support structures and expert groups. These structures and groups which played a fundamental role in developing the "acquis communautaire" have given way, under the present Programme, to a more streamlined management which not only ensures that the Community equal opportunities policy is more consistent but also contributes to it having a higher profile. Thus, under the present Programme, there are now only two expert groups to assist the Commission – a group of experts on "equality law" and a group of experts on "gender and employment". Each group is composed of relevant experts from all 15 Member States and two of the EEA countries (Iceland and Norway).

Also with a view to rationalising structures and resources, the Commission has established a technical assistance office (ANIMA) to provide help and expertise in the selection of projects to be funded, ensure the day-to-day follow-up of the projects funded, promote in networking among them, produce and disseminate, following the guidance given by the Commission, regular information on the implementation of the Programme and finally ensure the continuous monitoring of the initiatives funded by the Programme.

Also involved in the management of the programme at operational level, are a number of transnational partner organisations. The number of such organisations involved in the Programme's activities varies from one activity to another but what can be said is that these organisations have seen a positive development in each year of the implementation of the Programme. A database of organisations, potentially interested in becoming a partner organisation under the Programme has recently been developed and will be continuously enlarged and improved by the technical assistance office of the Programme. This database will in the second half of the Programme facilitate the project promoters' search for a matching partner organisation for their project.

The Programme's activities may be opened up to the participation of other countries as foreseen in Article 6 of the Council Decision. Two countries of the European Economic Area (EEA)- Iceland and Norway- have participated since the beginning of the Programme. The Commission has invited all 10 Central and Eastern European States (ACCEE) to participate and held a 2 day seminar in June 1997 to explain the procedures of the Programme. Six of them have already expressed their interest in adhering to the Programme. For three of them, (Rumania, Hungary and Lithuania) the legal and practical preparations are near completion at the time of drafting of this report.

In view of the challenges related to the enlargement of the European Union, the visibility of Community commitment to equality, as entailed in the Programme, will be, further developed in its second half.

I.4   The strategies developed under the Programme

The strategies tested in the course of the Programme's implementation are innovation, partnership and transfer of good practice. These three strategies have become a necessity for effective action and should therefore underpin all activities of the Programme. They are proving to be a fundamental contribution towards the achievement of the policy aims and in addition, a gain in terms of organisational learning for the project working teams.

In their applications, projects identified the elements of innovation in their proposals in a range of ways, ranging from the methodology tested to the activities foreseen. As regards partnership, it is intrinsically linked to the design of the Programme and it is implemented throughout by the variety of actors involved and by the co-operation modalities developed. Finally, regarding the transfer of good practice, the Programme is focussed on actions aimed at developing better ways of achieving equality and/or at disseminating practice which has already been demonstrated to be effective.

The added value of the Programme lies in the identification and exchange of information and experience on good practice in the field of equal opportunities for women and men among the key actors in this field (authorities, NGO's, social partners). The whole approach requires transnationality both as regards the partner organisations involved and the actions undertaken by the projects .

Compared with pure national or local based actions, the activities conducted in the frame of the Programme are valuable in contributing to actual change at operational level in local, national or European situations. This "built-in" added value is shown in the projects' results and will only be completely achieved as projects embark upon the dissemination stage of their actions.

The identification and exchange of information with the subsequent transfer of good practice on transnational level has worked satisfactorily for most project promoters. However, the more complex stage of international co-operation on designing and implementing measures,(i.e. the multilateral exchange of experience on good practice or the strategy for dissemination of results) was not initially a characteristic foreseen by all projects. The development of more elaborated transnational partnerships has therefore become one of the goals set for the second half of the programme.

II   ANALYSIS OF THE MID-TERM PROGRAMME'S ACTIVITIES AND RESULTS

In order to describe the Programme's implementation during its first half- life, activities and results are presented in section II.1 following the Programme's specific aims outlined in Article 3 of the Council Decision. The contribution of the Programme to the development of other Community policies and activities is presented in section II.2 of this report.

II.1   Analysis of the Programme's implementation per specific aim

- *II.1.1   General comments*

In 1996, the first year of the Programme, following an extensive mailing to interested organisations and multipliers as well as presentations of the Programme in almost all Member States the Commission received project proposals. These proposals were evaluated according to the eligibility criteria set out in the Decision. The Management Committee gave a favourable opinion on a list of projects presented by the Commission and subsequently 69 projects received contracts ending in June 1997. In actual fact only 67 received funding as two projects renounced the funding after their contracts were issued. 45 of the projects were foreseen as multi-annual. Thus, reports at the end of the first contractual period were limited to describing progress attained.

A call for proposals was published in the Official Journal to launch the second round of projects (budget exercise 1997). Following a selection procedure approved by the Management Committee, 71 projects were granted funding, with contracts up to June 1998. 37 of them proposed working on a multi-annual basis. At the time of drafting this report the projects funded during the second year are presenting their reports for the contractual period.

The same procedure has been applied for the third round of projects corresponding to the 1998 budget exercise. The Management Committee has agreed, at its meeting in June 1998, upon Commission proposal, the list of projects to be funded from July 1998 until June 1999. Contracts for those projects are being established at the time of drafting this report.

During the first two and a half years of the implementation of the Programme the representatives of the Member States met 10 times in the Management Committee fulfilling their role of assisting the Commission as foreseen in article 9 of the Decision. In addition, the members of the Committee were invited to several meetings of project promoters.

The criteria used for the selection of projects have followed the strategies of innovation, partnership and international exchange of good practice, as explained in previous section I.4 of this report.

As regards networking activities, 11 project promoter meetings have been held so far allowing for lively exchange of experience and information and thus facilitating further the transnationality of the projects initially selected. Two training sessions have been organised for project promoters with the objectives of firstly familiarising the promoters with the Community policy on equality, the role of the Programme within it and their own role within the Programme and, secondly providing the promoters with information and training on the financial rules and procedures for an optimal and efficient financial management of their projects.

The expert groups met in total eight times, there being once a year a joint meeting of the two networks to facilitate the preparation of joint tasks as requested by the Commission. Two round table discussions were organised on the subject of the assisting spouses of the self-employed[3]. One meeting with journalists took place on May 1998 to raise the awareness of the journalist profession and to brief them on a high level event at European level which was to mark the mid-term of the programme. This Congress and exhibition took place in September 1998 and was highly successful.

The themes of the 17 studies committed so far by the Programme were decided upon on the basis of the needs of the Programme in terms of scientific knowledge. Research Institutes responded to a call for study proposals launched in 1996 and to a restricted call for tender in 1997. The main selection criteria were the quality of the methodology and the qualifications of the research teams. Most of the selected studies cover all 15 Member States. Four of them were overview state-of-the-art studies on the major policy areas of the Programme: labour market, reconciliation, decision-making and the media. The Management Committee agreed, on its meeting of June 1998, on the subjects of the third call for studies. A restricted call for tender will shortly be made.

Dissemination strategy plays an important role, one of the major aims being the increase in visibility of Community action in the area of equality between women and men. For that purpose a variety of publications, each with a concrete target audience, has been produced. The quarterly Magazine (five numbers so far with, in all, 51.150 copies) is foreseen for the public at large, the information given covers policy issues related to equal opportunities. The internal bulletin (5 editions so far with, in all, 4.100 copies) is addressed to readers already involved in the Programme: project promoters, project partners, individuals or organisations with an expressed interest in the Programme. The Equality Quarterly News (six editions with, in all 8.100 copies) is more specifically designed for members of the legal professions across Europe. It presents current case law and the legislative situation both at European level and at national level, within the Member States. All publications are available in English and French, most of them also in German.

Several efforts have been made to further disseminate the activities included in the Programme: an annual Directory of projects has been produced (EN, FR and DE versions) in 1996 and 1997, with a total of 2,900 copies, which gives summary information of the projects supported each year[4]. A directory of products has been also produced (3,000 copies) showing the outcome of the projects funded during the first year of the Programme's implementation[5].

During the remaining part of the Programme, emphasis will be given to the organisation of thematic seminars in the Member States with the involvement of the Management Committee.

The mailing list of the Programme's publications contains about 8,200 entries including, apart from the Management and Advisory Committee members, Members of the European Parliament Committee on women's rights and Members of other European institutions, NGOs in the field of equality at European, national and regional level, equality agencies in the Member States, all project promoters and authors of studies under the present and past Community programmes on equal opportunities and, finally, individuals having expressed an interest in the Commission's activities on equal opportunities.

- *II.1.2 Gender Mainstreaming*

The adoption of the principle of integration as a primary driving force of the Programme is the result of the assessment of past achievements. The majority of actions undertaken to date promoting equal opportunities for women and men have been isolated measures. These specific actions were and still are important to combat inequality. However, there is a need for more general, complementary actions able to exert a serious influence on the orientation of general policies and on decision-makers. This combination defined by the Commission as the dual approach -specific action and mainstreaming-, is considered to be the most effective way to accomplish equality between women and men. On the basis of this observation, mainstreaming and its inherently global, exhaustive approach was adopted both as a guiding principle and as the primary, strategic objective of the Programme. Its implementation in practice opened the door to new actions and a whole series of previously unused initiatives at every level.

Two Studies were initiated in 1997[6] to improve the understanding of the success criteria of a mainstreaming strategy, the roles played by the different actors at the different levels, the monitoring mechanisms used and the development of progress indicators. These studies also seek to develop statistical models adopting a gender approach.

So far, 14 projects in total have targeted a range of different policy levels and policy areas, with the objective of promoting gender mainstreaming and developing tools and instruments for its implementation. Many projects within the Programme working within other fields of action contribute to the mainstreaming objective, particularly through partnership approaches, implicating key actors, networking, awareness-raising amongst decision-makers, contacts with politicians and development of tools, databases and guides.

From the experience gained so far, it can be seen that the context in which the project is anchored is a strong factor in defining the approach adopted. For example, local government provided the focus of the British Equal Opportunities Commission project[7], steered by a partnership of local government and equality organisations from four EU countries. In this case, the model approach to gender mainstreaming which was developed was grounded in the experience of and linked to the organisational interests of the partner institutions involved.

Planning and development, the use of working and living space, the use of time and the nature of urban and rural infrastructures have an impact on equal opportunities in complex but fundamental ways. In this respect, an ambitious project, co-ordinated by the European Network EuroFEM[8], and involving all Member States has been funded by the Programme. The project is operating in the fields of spatial planning, transport, housing and local development and is aiming at mainstreaming a gender perspective in planning and development. A "mainstreaming tool kit" for gender-sensitive project evaluation, which provides a list of good practices, has been produced based on case studies on projects in a number of European countries.

The Women's Talent Bank,[9] set up by the European Women's Lobby, has developed new tools designed to facilitate the integration of equality in all policies and actions. This is a database containing thousands of names of women experts in all the areas of competence covered by the Community policies. This new information source is being made available to European and other institutions to allow decision and policy-making processes, based on both male and female expertise.

Following the adoption of the Decision establishing mainstreaming as the guiding principle and strategic objective of the Programme, a Communication was adopted in February 1996 giving to gender mainstreaming the rank of a Community policy[10].

Gender mainstreaming is a completely new approach to equality between women and men. It requires the mobilisation of all policy areas and actors, including those not familiar with equality issues . It also requires a cultural change in mentality and behaviour. After only two and a half years of project activity, specific research and networking at European level, gender mainstreaming remains a concept in need of further development. The novelty and complexity of the concept means that the learning process, which has only started, must continue and develop both for projects implementation and for those making policy decisions.

- *II.1.3 Mobilisation for equality*

The experience of previous Community equal opportunities activities and programmes has shown that the commitment and involvement of the "traditional" equality actors (national equality agencies, women's NGOs) is not enough to achieve a fully equal European society and that a further mobilisation of all key actors of economic and social life is required if the objective of equality between women and men is to be validly achieved.

It has become necessary to broaden the circle of actors and institutions acting to promote equality through a strategy designed to integrate equality in all actions and policies and to foster attitudes which are more favourable to equal opportunities between women and men. Awareness raising of all key actors such as trade unions, local and regional authorities is needed and it is being done in the frame of the Programme's activities.

The Programme has so far supported 30 projects primarily addressing this objective, which have taken onboard the mobilisation of key actors in their fields of action and influencing public opinion. Their main activities aim to: a) raise awareness and change attitudes among key policy-makers and opinion-leaders; b) create leaders in social and economic sectors of society; and c) create own responsibility for social change and gradually build a critical mass of opinion and actions in favour of equal opportunities.

By establishing selection criteria, such as mentioning explicitly the importance of associating economic and social actors, or of associating men, particularly in managerial positions, by encouraging new and strong partnership and by defining the priority actors, as set up in the Annex to the Decision (social partners, non-governmental organisations, local authorities), the Commission has ensured the presence of new actors within the Programme.

Building up expertise and changing policies in the area of equality within social partner-institutions requires multiple actions, which targets a change of policies and attitudes in collective bargaining. Awareness raising and training of negotiators, learning and developing a gender approach is one of the main methods for the mobilisation of the social partners present in the Programme. The project EURO-FIET[11] involves the social partners, working in commercial, clerical, professional and technical sectors with the trade unions in the metal industries (IG Metal and FIM CISL).

Companies such as the Italian Railway company Ferrovia Nord Milano, the Credito Italiano Bank and bodies such as trade associations and chambers of commerce originating from Spain, Italy, Germany and France are present in the Programme as leading organisations.

Social partners, such as the European Trade Union Confederation (ETUC), the French trade union CFDT, the German 'Beamtenbund', a trade union organisation in the public service, and the Swedish energy company Sydkraft are leading important projects. These categories of actors are also mobilised as national and transnational partners in a large number of other projects.

To enhance further the participation of the social partners as priority actors of the Programme, and with a view to encourage them to co-operate on joint initiatives in the area of equal opportunities, an information meeting was organised in Brussels on 5th February 1998, with UNICE, ETUC and CEEP -the Union level employer and labour organisations at European level.

The mobilisation on new actors is directly linked with a shift in mentalities and attitudes. Working in the spirit of the "Charter on women in the Media"[12] adopted in May 1995, several radio and TV companies have become actively involved in the Programme.

Projects have made good use of many different contexts to involve and inform key local and national actors in their work. Lobbying, networking, informing and training have all been used. Manifestos, databases, videos, seminars, newsletters and conferences have formed the basis of information strategies. The information and dissemination strategies of projects have focused on representatives of major institutions as well as general public opinion, and the advantages of equal opportunities to these institutions in a changing world have been stressed.

In the next phase of the Programme, continuation of these activities, together with new approaches and policies, will be developed and implemented. A wider involvement particularly of men in key positions in trade unions, enterprises or in local and regional authorities with a higher level of awareness of equality must feature amongst the priorities to secure successful mobilisation in the remaining half of the Programme.

- *II.1.4 Equality in a changing economy*

At the Essen summit, in December 1994, equality of opportunity between women and men was identified as a 'paramount task of the European Union and its Member States' and a requirement for the continued development of the internal market. The promotion of equal opportunities has since then been at the heart of economic planning and policy at European level.

The objective of equality between women and men in the labour market has been considerably strengthened over the last few years. More and more companies are capitalising on diversity in the workforce. Although women have accounted for the large majority of the new jobs created in the last decade, their employment rate is still at a much lower level than men's. Furthermore, the labour market remains highly segregated. Women are rarely represented in top-level management position. Women also tend to be concentrated in part-time or temporary work and homework.

20 transnational projects have developed activities focusing primarily on employment and working life. Key areas of action within this objective are the access of women to male dominated sectors and professions and mentoring programmes tackling the glass ceiling at managerial level. Other central themes explored by projects are positive action, flexibility, organisational change, and women's entrepreneurship. In the field of education, the focus has been mainly on pilot actions and good practice examples concerned with specific target groups, such as migrant women and their inclusion in the labour market and society as a whole. Particular attention has been paid at avoiding any overlapping with the European Social Fund initiatives and with the Community actions in the field of education and training (Leonardo and Socrates programmes).

The advancement of women's entrepreneurship has been reflected by mainstream organisations such as chambers of commerce[13] and other enterprises in a project supported by the Programme. As an example, the Credito Italiano Bank project[14], in collaboration with partners in the UK, Belgium, and Portugal, is developing specific facilities for women's enterprises, as a follow-up on a survey on women's needs for financial tools such as leasing, project financing and electronic banking.

The Programme has so far launched six studies in this area. One is an overview of state of the art studies on women in the labour market[15]; another is a study on self-employed workers and their assisting spouses[16]. This last study has been the basis of the organisation of two round tables, in 1997 on the assisting spouses of the self-employed. Also in 1997, two studies[17][18], an inventory of indicators for the gender assessment of employment and labour market policies and the earning differentials between men and women based on the results of the Eurostat's structure of earning survey – were launched and are presently underway.

Gender equality in the labour market cannot be reached effectively from the outside. The involvement of the key players to ensure a better gender equality is needed. The integration of equality in enterprises is much more successful in cases where actions are linked directly to the needs of the enterprise and decisions are agreed jointly by trade unions and management. As already mentioned, the Programme has taken in a great number of key actors in this field, such as trade unions, national and multinational enterprises, commercial chambers, working in collaboration with experienced research centres and universities.

A good example of mobilising different actors to improve the access of women pursuing a career in science, technology and industry in the energy sector is the project led by the Swedish company Sydkraft[19], bringing together Swedish and Irish social partners and enterprises. This project is making a strong effort to change policies and mentalities, putting equal opportunities on the agenda in boardrooms, proposing specific policies and awareness raising activities.

Examples of transferring good practice as well as a wide mobilisation of actors are also provided in the field of flexibility in work organisation. This is usually regarded as an economic necessity in today's changing world of employment. The approach taken in the Programme is that unions and employers can work together to introduce work flexibility which benefits both employers and employees. Positive models of flexibility from various Member States are being collected in several projects, such as a joint UK and Dutch trade union project, led by the UK Trades Union Congress[20]. This project is successfully influencing national debate on flexible working hours by showing positive and manageable examples of workplace flexibility.

A special dossier within the Programme's periodical, "The Magazine"[21], was dedicated to the Commission's Green Paper 'partnership for a new organisation of work' in December 1997. The dossier included an overview on projects working on questions linked to the Commission Green Paper. The programme has, in this way, contributed in the debate and collection of information launched by the Green Paper.

Under the Luxembourg Presidency, in the second semester of 1997, a European Conference took place on the equality dimension of the new ways of work organisation[22], with the support of the Programme. Several successful examples of projects funded by the Programme were presented at the Conference. The proceedings of the Conference have been published with the support of the Programme.

Traditional role expectations and other (indirect) discriminatory mechanisms in corporate culture still prevent women from participating in the labour market on an equal footing. This long overlooked aspect of gender inequality in the labour market can be effectively combated by the so called "mentoring" approach, mobilising management in enterprise, public administration and personnel departments in favour of a new generation of women managers. The Programme supports pilot actions and the transfer of examples of good practice in this field, focusing in particular on higher levels of management.

In particular, an overall research action is being carried out by the Deutsches Jugendinstitut[23], tracking down existing mentoring projects all over Europe and initiating mentoring activities in Member States where the mentoring approach is not yet implemented. It is clear from project results so far, that mentoring is not only an extremely useful experience for both mentors and mentorees, but also has a potential impact on management policies and can contribute to changes in corporate culture.

Labour market policies and innovations in work organisation and in society at large are often implemented without full consideration of the implications for gender equality. Action based research tools and models developed under the Programme aim to influence positively management practices towards more gender consciousness. Concrete and result oriented policy tools to pursue change in the industry are produced by transnational projects working in this area, like the French CFDT project,[24], such as: analytic and diagnostic tools for gender audits, guidelines and handbooks for incorporating gender issues in collective bargaining

Progress is also being made in the field of women in enterprise, science and technology at senior level. The WITEC-database[25] covering Belgium, Spain, Germany, Sweden, Denmark and the Netherlands aims to make a contribution to overcome the under-representation of women in male dominated sectors and professions showing an extensive list of senior female scientists and technologists in almost every scientific domain.

Within the regular project promoters' meeting, co-ordinating workshops have been organised with the aim of creating interconnections between projects and collaboration in this field. Two special bulletins have been published in this area; one on trends in women's employment during the 1990s in April 1997[26] and a second one on Gender and Working time in the 1990s in December 1997[27].

The European Employment Strategy provides new incentives to increase activities, in particular focusing on reversing the under-representation of women in certain economic sectors and occupations and their over-representation in others. Another important area identified for increased activity is the recognition and promotion of women's entrepreneurship and its contribution to society. These aspects, directly connected with the employment guidelines on equal opportunities between women and men, will be reinforced both by projects and other activities within the framework of the Programme in its second half.

Priority will be given to projects and activities focusing on changes made in the labour market and with a potential impact on policies at national and European level The results of these projects as well as of related work conducted by the Programme's expert groups have the potential to contribute to further development of the Employment Guidelines.

- *II.1.5 Reconciling work and family*

This objective deals with the increasing diversity in both the workplace and family life and the changes in the relationship between the two. In order to harness the economic potential of women, and their desire to enter, or re-enter, the labour market, policies allowing for a better reconciliation of work and family life must be further pursued. Household structures and relationships are moving towards more 'non-traditional' households as a result of rapid change. There is, however, still a wide diversity of situations in the Member States and this makes, on the one hand the actions at European level complex but, on the other hand, the exchange of experiences and good practice more meaningful.

Developing policies and practices for a better reconciliation of work and family life is one of the main challenges of the Programme. This calls for information and awareness raising activities targeted both at men and women, employers and employees. Projects have taken up policy, information and awareness raising activities.

One major state of the art review on the reconciliation of work and family life for men and women was completed in June 1997. The study[28] focuses on the quality of care services, as well as on flexible work as a means of reconciling work and family life, and includes an analysis of the potential risk of an increase in precariousness of women's work.

12 projects have been funded by the Programme in the first two years. They primarily focus on the reconciliation of work and family and cover important subjects such as the interaction of opportunities for and access to paid work with other aspects of family, care, leisure and civic life. Projects also deal with the gender roles in families and the sharing of responsibilities within the home, with advising and supporting employees with care responsibilities and with the important subject of out-of-school childcare.

Several projects in this area focus on measures and policies benefiting both employers and employees. The business case for promoting flexible working to allow employees to reconcile their work and family life, in terms of recruitment and retention of staff, increased motivation, decreased absence and staff turnover, is clearly shown in the projects.

Model solutions and training materials are the practical outcomes of case studies and joint transnational pilot actions. The professional pilots in the UK, Sweden, Norway and Denmark form the sample population for a research report and an action guide on supporting employees with caring responsibilities, produced by the UK based project "Children in Scotland"[29]. Good practice examples concerning the so called 'time banks', as developed in several Italian cities, are being used to develop similar activities in the "Salud y Familia"[30] project in Barcelona, targeting the use of time within the family and setting up a mutual support system.

A number of projects have gone further in considering the interests and motivation of men. The City of Reykjavik[31] has looked in depth at what motivates men to take parental leave and to what else can be done to further promote among men the take-up of paternity leave. A TV documentary, in which the take up of paternity leave by men is monitored throughout the period of leave, served to generate a wider debate in Iceland on gender roles and will be also broadcast in other European countries.

Another example of mobilising both women and men is provided by the Belgian Bond van Grote en Jonge Gezinnen[32], offering practical and attractive training materials for groups discussing gender roles within the family. The materials, having already generated a wide debate in Belgium, have now been produced in a Spanish version and are being used in Spanish discussion groups on a wide scale. The Portuguese Graal project[33] and the project by the Women's Institute in the Spanish Basque region[34], also mobilise men for discussions and training sessions. These examples of transnational exchange of innovation and good practice provide a good testimony on the European added value of the projects supported by the Programme.

The two expert groups of the Programme produced a joint report entitled "Care in Europe"[35] in March 1998 which provides an overview of the situation in Europe as regards the care of children as well as dependant elderly relatives (see section II.2.2).

> In view of demographic trends, identifying good practice in the field of care and, in particular, reinforcing the participation of men in care activities (both within the family and within the care services sector) will become an important issue in the coming years of the Programme.
>
> In addition, the question of how to reconcile work and family life has until now mainly been addressed by studies and projects in larger companies. In many respects working conditions in micro and small companies are very different from those in larger companies; consequently, questions concerning reconciling work and family life in micro and small companies should also be addressed in a specific manner within the remaining half of the Programme. Given the fact that the development of family- friendly working policies together with a better reconciliation of family and working life have been identified as important issues in the Employment Guidelines, the results of these projects have the potential to support the future development of the Employment Guidelines.

- *II.1.6 Gender balance in decision-making*

Promoting a gender balance in decision-making is one of the key objectives of the Programme. Although there is nowadays wide recognition of the importance of a balanced representation of women and men in decision-making, women are still underrepresented in politics, public and private institutions and generally in posts where decisions are taken. In many European countries political and policy structures are in the process of change. This change, brought about by political and economic crises, creates an opportunity to accelerate the increase of women in decision-making processes. Social changes are leading to a further acknowledgement that gender balance in all sectors of society is not anymore a women's demand, but an unavoidable feature of a modern, democratic society.

Solid information on women's positions at all levels and in all sectors of the decision making processes is crucial in order to mobilise different actors for action. The Commission has improved existing knowledge on this issue by conducting, in the framework of the Programme, a European wide overview state of the art study on women in political, economic and social decision-making in Europe[36] in 1996.

As regards political decision-making, the European wide database, created by the Frauen Computer Zentrum, in the framework of the Programme,[37] enables strategies or campaigns to be developed, thereby raising awareness, on the actual situation, on progress made and on the continuing gaps and the differences between Member States. The availability of up-to date data on women in political decision-making is considered one of the main results achieved by the Programme and the data provided have already been used in the 1997 Annual Report on equal opportunities in the European Union.

One more study on the impact of electoral systems on women's representation in Parliaments was launched in 1997[38] and is underway.

A total of 16 projects have developed a large spectrum of activities promoting a gender balance in decision-making, especially in politics. Among them is the setting up and expansion of European networks of women politicians;[39] three major European conferences[40]; awareness raising campaigns for the presence of women in politics[41]; one exchange programme between Swedish and Spanish politicians[42], several capacity building and training activities for women in leadership[43], and a great number of publications and transnational meetings.

Workshops for projects in this area were organised in all project promoters' meetings with the aim of creating links and strengthening collaboration in this field. A special dossier in the Programme's magazine in July 1997[44] was dedicated to the gender balance in decision making giving information on progress made by the projects. A thematic meeting was organised by the Programme in January 1998, with the presence of European Parliament members, project promoters and experts. They discussed new concepts, strategies and possible actions which could be undertaken to achieve more balanced results in the coming European Parliament elections.

Projects take on experiences from different levels of decision-making (local, national and European) and from different Member States. This process has been facilitated thanks to the already existing European instruments and tools, such as the Council Recommendation[45], the Declaration of Athens[46], the Charter of Rome[47] and the Guide "How to create a gender balance in decision-making"[48] produced in the frame of the previous Programmes on equal opportunities.

It is no longer in question that women should enter the political arena. New, more qualitative questions are being raised. Experience shows that the equal representation of women and men in decision making provokes organisational changes and more chances for mainstreaming gender in all policies. It is visible that more and more projects dealing with women in decision-making are incorporating such strategy in their activities.

The Danish National Women's Council, within the framework of the Programme, has systematically evaluated local electoral campaigns in Denmark[49]. The evaluation of the data, which also took into account data from Sweden, indicates that it is, in particular, in local campaigns, where involving more women is effective in generating more gender balanced results. Evaluation of the Swedish electoral campaigns shows that support from the top of the political system is a crucial element in order to achieve results. A strong organisation, preferably across party lines, has also been found essential.

Several projects can be considered as examples of dissemination of good practice, such as the information measures undertaken by Regimprensa[50], a regional newspaper in the Lisbon region. It mobilised actors in local communities in order to increase the number of women in local decision-making positions. It is also an example of how the regional press can play an important role in raising awareness on women's presence in politics.

Good practice on leadership training and empowerment approaches has been built up and transferred during this stage of the Programme. These activities are designed not only to improve the access of women to decision-making positions, but also to ensure, in a demanding situation, women's successful continuance in those positions. The results of leadership training indicate that this is an effective additional instrument in order to empower women.

In order to increase women's participation at all levels of decision-making and in all sectors of society, priority will be given, during the second half of the Programme, to the sectors of society such as culture, the media and environment and types of strategies such as the development of regulatory measures, public campaigns and quota systems which are not yet well analysed, for both quantitative and qualitative study. The Programme will continue to monitor women's position at the political decision-making level in local, regional, national and European institutions and will strengthen co-operation with other institutions in this field.

- *II.1.7 Exercising equality rights*

At European level, formal equal rights through legislation and European Court of Justice case law collectively constitute a unique and much acknowledged model. Yet, in the different Member States, there is an unawareness of, or least an unfamiliarity with, the legislation and the case law, both by the final beneficiaries thereof and by a majority of professionals working in this field. This apparent contradiction fully justifies the efforts of the Programme in this area.

Two lines of action have been defined in the Programme. First, a set of activities aimed at removing the obstacles to the effective application of Community legislation, and a second aimed at improving the quality and quantity of information on equality rights, focusing in particular on women and on those practising in the legal professions.

As far as equal pay for work of equal value is concerned, several actions have been undertaken to facilitate the implementation of this basic principle of Community law. They include conferences, seminars and exchange of projects[51] which demonstrate the extent to which exercising equality rights must be reinforced, both before the courts and elsewhere, using new methods and mechanisms. A Code of Conduct[52] concerning the application of equal pay, published and widely distributed by the Commission, constitutes a reference tool in this area.

The conference organised in Dublin on 25 November 1996[53] – supported by the Programme - confirmed that the causes of today's pay gaps are rooted both in job evaluation systems and in the difficulties concerning effective sanctions against pay discrimination.

Two transnational projects have also worked on the theme of equal pay: the ETUC[54]project has launched a series of national conferences aimed at raising awareness among trade union negotiators and at providing information on the subject of pay discrimination for their work on collective agreements. With the Belgian Ministry of Employment and Labour, and the "classification and remuneration" project[55], there has been a move away from the strictly legal domain to identify other methods which could put an end to wage discrimination. The results have shed light on the opportunities, existing in Member States, in favour of equal pay outside the legal framework. The "good practices" identified by the project consisted of actions and measures concerning job evaluation systems used to eliminate or avoid discrimination based on sex which exist in current employment practice, whether intentionally or otherwise.

Two particular questions have given rise to debate and exchange of views within in the framework of the Programme at European level: the situation regarding the spouses of self-employed workers and the individualisation of social and fiscal rights:

- Two round tables on assisting spouses were held during the first half of 1997. The proceeding has been published[56] and disseminated in order to raise awareness about this issue. The need to plan actions outside the scope of the legal framework in order to make the work of these spouses more visible through i.e. awareness-raising, training, registration, was identified as an important conclusion thereof.

- A seminar was held in Paris in October 1997[57] on individualisation of rights providing a clearer picture of the different approaches to social protection and taxation systems in the Member States.

Information provided directly to women on their rights is a long-term task, which must be carried out through a variety of channels. The information policy developed within the Programme is designed to secure the dissemination and popularisation of information on women's rights through different publications. The Magazine includes a section dedicated to news on equality rights in Europe. Additionally, an 8-page supplement to the magazine is periodically dedicated to the work of the group of experts on equality law.

The Greek project entitled 'Watch for Women's Rights'[58] illustrates in very concrete terms the need for the information and support, both crucial for the effective application of women's rights. The low level of litigation linked to sex discrimination in Southern Europe is more a reflection of the limited knowledge of these rights and the absence of suitable support structures than of a real absence of discrimination. On the basis of this consideration, the project has developed a multi-dimensional action including, in particular, support to facilitate the starting of legal procedures. The results underline women's lack of understanding of their rights and their need for suitable legal counselling.

The information and awareness-raising project led by the Spanish agency for equality, "Instituto de la Mujer"[59] also identifies this crucial need of information. Providing information on Community law and raising awareness amongst the social partners and the members of the legal professions, the project is adapting and transferring existing mechanisms and measures from Member States where information mechanisms are more developed.

The need for a reinforcement of conditions, under which equality rights are exercised, is underlined by the growing importance of European law in everyday life of European citizens, both male and female. Information on rights and other actions must be founded upon expertise, which is to be recognised by and targeted at the members of the legal profession, and subsequently implemented. In this regard, it is also a question of implementing gender mainstreaming in all areas of law. Awareness-raising campaigns on equality, aimed at the members of the legal profession practising in all areas, need to be developed and implemented in the second half of the Programme.

II.2 The role of the Programme within the Community policies and activities

- *II.2.1 General comments*

The Programme has contributed to putting gender equality at the highest level of the political agenda of the EU and stimulated debate on the importance of equality during the design and development of major Community policies. More concretely, the Programme has paved the way to improving the profile and the scope of the principle of equality at European level (the Treaty of Amsterdam, the equality legislation). The mainstreaming approach has been particularly successful, incorporating the objective of equality between women and men in the labour market at the heart of the European Employment Strategy and of the current proposal of the Commission for the Structural Funds' reform (2000–2006).

What follows is an illustration of the relevance of the Programme's objectives in different Community developments and policies.

- *II.2.2 The Mainstreaming Strategy*

A methodological approach, developed within the framework of the Programme, has been adopted with a view to implementing the gender mainstreaming strategy within the Commission. It involves the close co-operation of all the services, the appointment of responsible officials at a high level under the co-ordination of the services in charge of the Programme, awareness-raising and training, development of practical tools and guidelines and regular monitoring and evaluation of progress.

The Community commitment to gender mainstreaming has been decisively underpinned by the Treaty of Amsterdam[60], which lists the promotion of equality between women and men among the Community objectives and as a horizontal concern, in Articles 2 and 3. The integration of these principles into the Treaty demonstrates the effectiveness of mainstreaming and of mobilising all actors in political and social life to achieving equality. The commitment to promoting equality in all Community policies, clearly stated in the new Treaty, provides a solid basis for action on gender mainstreaming at Community level.

Two years after the adoption of the Commission Communication[61] on mainstreaming, a Progress Report[62] was adopted on 4 March 1998 on the implementation of the gender mainstreaming policy. Considerable results have been reached so far and are well documented in the Progress Report in the fields of development co-operation and external relations, in the sector of information and personnel policies, in policies related to education training and youth. In the research policy there has also been a major surge to improve the participation of women.

Two European networks of women politicians were supported by the Programme: the network of elected women at local and regional level of the Council of European Municipalities and Regions (CEMR)[63], and the Conference of Committees on Equality of National Parliaments (CCEO),[64] initiated by the Belgian Senate. They succeeding in mobilising their members on issues related to the Intergovernmental Conference and to the inclusion of equality in the new draft Treaty and have also facilitated equality policies in their respective institutions, in particular on issues related to the objectives of the Programme. The European network for women (EUDIF)[65] funded by the Programme sought to promote debate on equality among NGOs during the IGC.

The gender mainstreaming strategy of the Commission will be further developed in the second half of the programme period through a training and awareness-raising programme. In line with new Article 3 of the Amsterdam Treaty, Commission procedures and regulations will be closely examined, with a view to improving the gender balance in all its decision-making and advisory structures and to ensuring that all Commission legal proposals and non-legal activities comply with the Treaty obligation to promote equality between women and men.

- *II.2.3   The European Employment Strategy*

The 1998 Employment Guidelines adopted by the Council in December 1997[66] inserted the equal opportunity dimension at the heart of European Employment Strategy. Equality is now one of the priorities which should underpin national employment policies. Member States have to undertake policies aimed at tackling gender gaps, at enabling women and men to reconcile work and family life, and at facilitating women and men to return to work after an absence.

The Community Programme on equal opportunities has so far made a significant contribution to the justification, formulation and development of the equality pillar in the employment guidelines. The evidence collected through different research and action projects has shown that important gender gaps remain in the labour market, and that the position of women as compared to men is not yet equal. The experience gained with the implementation of the Programme has been essential in support of the inclusion of the equal opportunities pillar in the employment guidelines.

The trends on women's position in the labour market have been confirmed by the research done by the "Gender and Employment" expert group of the Programme. This group has produced a study[67] on employment and working time policies in Europe, which served to launch the debate on this issue.

In 1997, a major state of the art research on women and the labour market was completed in the frame of the programme and published in July 1998[68]. This study has served to identify the next steps in research.

The joint report "Care in Europe", produced in the framework of the Programme (see section II.1.5), served to prepare the Commission background document for the meeting of Ministers responsible for equal opportunities in Belfast, May 1998.

The Belfast meeting paved the way to the important declaration[69] made in June 1998 by the European Council in Cardiff where Member States agreed to strengthen gender mainstreaming in the employment guidelines and to encourage measures aiming at a better reconciliation of family and working life.

An in-depth gender assessment of the National Action Plans, which Member States were committed to submit to the Commission by virtue of the common employment strategy, was carried out by the Gender and Employment expert group in order to support the Commission in its preparations for the Joint Informal Council of Social Affairs and Equality Ministers in Innsbruck, July 1998.

> The Programme will, in its second half, continue providing documented information and models of good practice as regards the situation of women in the European labour market, analysing the annual National Action Plans from a gender perspective and thus contributing to strengthening the equality component of the Employment strategy.

- *II.2.4   The Structural Funds*

The Structural Funds are the Union's primary instruments for the achievement of economic and social cohesion. The gender mainstreaming approach developed by the Commission in the context of the Programme contributed greatly to developing further awareness of gender issues within all Commission services in charge of preparing the proposal for the reform of the Structural Funds.

The Commission proposal for the reform of the Structural Funds has very much taken into account the gender dimension. It includes the dual approach, both mainstreaming and specific measures. The integration of the mainstreaming strategy in the general and specific regulations of all the Funds will permeate the whole implementation process, from the programming phase to reporting. In addition, the support of specific measures such as combating unemployment, supporting returners to the labour market, access to entrepreneurship and reducing segregation in the labour market will have an important relevance for women's full integration in the labour market.

Without prejudging the results of the negotiation on this proposal within the Community institutions which is underway at the time of drafting this report, one can say without any doubt that equality between women and men is at the heart of Community priorities for the future of the Structural Funds.

A further collaboration and attuning with the Structural Funds and in particular with the European Social Fund will be sought in the second half of the Programme's period of implementation. In particular, the exchange of information and results among projects of the Programme and those funded by the ESF Community initiative NOW will be also reinforced. In the second half of the Programme it is envisaged to organise joint information and dissemination events in the Member States.

- *II.2.5   European Equality Legislation*

During the first two years of the implementation of the Programme, the Commission has continued its legislative work to complete the existing legal instruments in areas which until now had not yet been fully covered. During this period the Commission's proposal for a directive on the burden of proof[70] in cases of sex discrimination in the workplace, was adopted by the Council, after a lively discussion. This legislative instrument is designed to reinforce the conditions under which rights can be exercised, facilitating as it does litigation in cases of discrimination based on sex.

The relevance of equality has been further recognised in the Council Directive on the framework agreement on parental leave[71] concluded by the general cross-industry organisations UNICE, CEEP and ETUC which grants men and women an individual right to parental leave for at least three months, which can – in principle – not be transferred to the other parent. This right, conferred on men on an equal basis with women, has thereby the potential to contribute to a more equal share between women and men of family obligations. This incentive to men to take a more active part in care will thereby encourage the reduction of gender based stereotypes. The Programme has laid emphasis on projects which aim at the participation of men in care work[72].

A major Community legal instrument was adopted by the Council in 1996, the Recommendation on the balanced participation of women and men in the decision-making process[73]. In May 1998 a seminar for government representatives was held within the framework of the Programme to discuss the progress made in the Member States regarding the implementation of this Recommendation and to facilitate in this way the Commission monitoring of the follow-up of the Recommendation.

The group of experts on equality law is of fundamental assistance to the Commission in monitoring developments at Member State level in the area of equality rights. The group produces and submits to the Commission an annual report giving a panoramic view of the application of equality rights across the Union. Apart from the information provided on legislative and judicial developments at Member State and European level, it offers an analysis of current developments and a "gender proofing" of law and legal procedures, which cannot be found elsewhere. This report is a reference tool for legal professionals in all Member States. Information about current case law and the legislative situation in Europe and within Member States is provided through Equality Quarterly News.

During its second half, the Programme will continue monitoring the implementation of the European equality legislation at national level as well as following developments in national law and national legal procedures. Special efforts will be made to disseminate equality law and procedures among the legal professionals in the candidate countries.

Notes

[1] Hereinafter referred to as "the Programme"

[2] Council Decision (95/593/EC), OJ No L 335, 30.12.95, p. 37

[3] See endnote 56 below

[4] European Commission, Medium-term Community Action Programme on Equal Opportunities for Women and Men, "Directory of Projects 1996" and "Directory of Projects 1997"

[5] European Commission, Medium-term Community Action Programme on Equal Opportunities for Women and Men, "Directory of Projects – Year 1"

[6] Centre for Regional Economic and Social Research (CRESR), "Criteria for success of a "Mainstreaming" approach to gender equality", SEDEP (Service de développement et d'évaluation de programmes de formation), "Mechanisms and indicators in the monitoring of the mainstreaming process", Research Programme 1997/98

[7] Equal Opportunities Commission, "Mainstreaming Gender Equality in Local Government", 1996 (UK1/52/96)

[8] EuroFEM, "Development of infrastructure for everyday life – Evaluation of EuroFEM projects", 1996 (FN1/47/96) – 1997 (FNa/47/97)

[9] European Women's Lobby, "Women's Talent Bank", 1996 (EUR5/66/96) – 1997 (EURa/66/97)

[10] "Incorporating equal opportunities for women and men into all Community policies and activities" (COM(96)67 final) of 21.2.1996

[11] Euro-Fiet: European Organisation of the International Federation of Commercial Clerical, Professional and Technical Employees, "Transnational Women's Network in the Private Services Sector – Mainstreaming in the Social Dialogue", 1997 (EURa/98/97)

[12] Charter for Equal Opportunities for Women in Broadcasting, adopted by European broadcasting organisations on the occasion of the EBU/EC Conference on 5 May 1995

[13] Camara de Comercio e Industria de Toledo, "INNOVADONNA – the dynamism and internationalisation of women's entrepreneurial activity", 1997 (ESb/80/97)

[14] Credito Italiano Bruxelles – A.I.D.D.A., "W.E.PRO – Access to credit for women entrepreneurs in SMEs. Globalisation and international trade", 1997 (ITb/87/97)

[15] see endnote 10

[16] EIM Small business research and consultancy, "Self-employed workers and assisting spouses", Research Programme 1996/97

[17] ENGENDER asbl, "Inventory of indicators for the gender assessment of employment and labour market policies", Research Programme 1997/98;

[18] APPLICA sprl, "Earning differentials between men and women based on the results of the Eurostat structure of earning survey", Research Programme 1997/98

[19] Sydkraft AB, "ENEQO: An overview of Equal Opportunities in the Energy Sector", 1997 (SWb/95/97)

[20] Trades Union Congress, "Gender and Flexibility: the organisation of work and time – an action programme", 1997 (UKb/97/97)

[21] European Commission, "Equal Opportunities Magazine" no. 3 – December 1997

[22] International Conference, "Organisation du Travail", organised by the Luxembourg Presidency, 23 October 1997, Luxembourg

[23] Deutsches Jugendinstitut e.V., "Mentoring on women in Europe – Research on existing mentoring and counselling projects in Europe and evaluation of examples of good practice", 1996 (DE2/06/96) – 1997 (DEb/06/97)

[24] Confédération Française Démocratique du Travail (CFDT), "Bargaining for equal opportunities", 1997 (FRb/82/97)

[25] WITEC, "Development of a database of Women experts in science, engineering and technology on the World Wide Web", 1996 (EUR5/67/96)

[26] European Commission, "Equal Opportunities Magazine", no. 1 - April 1997

[27] European Commission, "Equal Opportunities Magazine", no. 3 – December 1997

[28] Thomas Coram Research Unit (TCRU) Institute of Education, University of London, "Overview state of the art study on reconciliation of work and family life for men and women and the quality of care services", Research Programme 1996/97

[29] Children in Scotland, "Taking account of children and families in the environment structure and organisation of the workplace: Promoting Public Sector Action", 1996 (UK2/53/96) – 1997 (UKb/53/97)

[30] Asociación Salud y Familia, "Sharing : promoting a better distribution of time between women and men", 1997 (ESb/79/97)

[31] Council of Reykjavik – Committee on gender equality in Reykjavik, "Fathers on Paternity Leave", 1996 (IC2/68/96) – 1997 (ICb/68/97)

[32] Bond van Grote en van Jonge Gezinnen, "European family dialogue leading to a new division of labour between women and men in the European family", (B1/01/96) – 1997 (Bb/01/97)

[33] GRAAL, "Towards an active society", 1996 (PT2/45/96) – 1997 (PTb/45/97)

[34] EMAKUNDE/ Instituto Vasco de la Mujer, "AUKERA: Shared responsibility for domestic tasks of women and men", 1997 (ESb/81/97)

[35] Francesca Bettio, Sacha Prechal, Salvatore Bimonte, Silvana Giorgi,: "Care in Europe", Joint Report of the "Gender and Employment" and the "Gender and Law" network of experts, Equal Opportunities Unit, DG V, of the European Commission, March 1998

[36] University of Southampton, Department of Politics, "State of the art study of research on the quantity and quality of women's participation in European political, social and economic decision-making", Research Programme 1996/97

[37] Frauen Computer Zentrum Berlin, "European Database – Women in decision-making", 1996 (DE5/19/96) – 1997 (DEc/14/97)

[38] P & D Analytics, "Electoral Systems: a Gender Impact Assessment", Research Programme 1997/998

[39] See endnotes 5 and 6

[40] AFEM, (Association des Femmes de l'Europe Méridionale), "Concerted, specific strategies to promote women's access to decision-making in Southern Europe", 1996 (FR3/28/96) – 1997 (FRc/28/97) and überpartiliche Frauen initiative – Berlin, Stadt der Frauen e.V., "Citizen's Union: strategies and co-operation for Europe in the year 2000", 1997 (DEa/71/97)

[41] National Women's Council of Ireland, "Getting the balance right: A quality approach to gender equality in decision-making", 1996 (IRL3/32/96) – 1997 IRLc/32/97)

[42] Landstingsförbundet, "Network of Swedish and Spanish politicians at the regional level" 1996 (SW3/50/96)

[43] Women of the North West Ltd., "Moygownah – Women in Leadership", 1997 (IRLc/84/97) Technische Universität Berlin, "Preparing women to lead: support for a new generation of women managers", 1997 (DEc/78/97)

[44] European Commission, "Equal Opportunities Magazine", no. 2 – July 1997

[45] Council Recommendation (96/694/EC) of 2 December 1996 on the balanced participation of women and men in the decision-making process. OJ L 319/11 of 10.12.96.

[46] "Declaration of Athens" signed on 3 November 1992 by women holding senior positions from each of the EC Member States, the EFTA, as well as from East European countries and from the EP, the Council of Europe and the United Nations, see "Equal Opportunities for Women and Men in the EU 1996" (CE-98-96-566-EN) p. 86

[47] "Charter of Rome" signed on 18 May 1996 by women ministers of 13 Member States at the "Women for the renewal of politics and society" conference in Rome, published in "How to create a gender balance in decision-making", see reference footnote 59, p. 73

[48] "How to create a gender balance in decision-making", a guide to implementing policies for increasing the participation of women in political decision-making by Monique Leijenaar in collaboration with the European experts network "Women in decision-making (CE-01-96-131-EN-C)

[49] Danske Kvinders Nationalrad, "Parity Democracy: gender balanced composition of municipal and county councils", (DKc/70/97)

[50] Regimpresa CRL, "Actors in local politics. When the essential issues become the women's cause", 1996 (PT4/46/96) – 1997 (PTc/46/97)

[51] see endnotes 53, 54 and 55.

[52] A Code of Practice on the Implementation of Equal Pay for Work of Equal Value for Women and Men, COM (96) 336 final

[53] Expert Seminar on Equal Pay for Work of Equal Value, organised by the Equality Employment Agency (EEA) of Ireland on 25 November 1996 to launch the Commission's Code of Practice on Equal Pay for Work of Equal Value

[54] European Trade Union Confederation (ETUC), "Equal pay for work of equal value", 1996 (EUR2/61/96)

[55] Ministerie van Tewerkstelling en Arbeid – Dienst Gelijke Kansen, "From classification to remuneration", 1996 (B2/02/96) – 1997 (Bb/02/97)

[56] European Commission, Directorate-General for Employment, Industrial Relations and Social Affairs, Unit V/D/5, "Assisting spouses of the self-employed – Report of the two round tables organised by the European Commission in Brussels on 7 February and 23 and 24 June 1997".

[57] Seminar "Individualisation des droits, sécurité sociale et égalité des chances entres hommes et femme", organised by the University of Nanterre on 9-11 October 1997, Paris

[58] Citizens for Athens, "Watch for Women's Rights in Athens", 1996 – (EL4/7/96) – 1997 (ELb/17/97)

[59] Instituto de la Mujer, "Equal opportunities between women and men on the labour market", 1996 (ES2/22/96) – 1997 (ESb/22/97)

[60] Treaty of Amsterdam amending the Treaty on European Union, the Treaties establishing the European Communities and certain related acts, signed at Amsterdam, 2 October 1997 (97/C 340), OJ No. C 340, 10.11.97, p.1

[61] See endnote 10

[62] Progress Report from the Commission on the follow-up of the Communication: "Incorporating equal opportunities for women and men into all Community policies and activities" (COM (1998) 122 final

[63] Council of European Municipalities and Regions (CEMR), "Development of a European network of local and regional women politicians", 1996 (EUR 3/63/96) – 1997 (EUR c/63/97)

[64] Belgische Senaat, "Network of Equal Opportunities Committees of National Parliaments in the EU Member States and the Committee on Women's Rights of the European Parliament"(CCEO), 1996 (B3/03/96) – 1997 (Bc/03/97)

[65] EUDIF, "Citizens in the Europe of equal representation", 1996 (EUR 4/65/96) – 1997 (EUR d/65/97)

[66] Council Resolution of 15 December 1997 on the 1998 Employment Guidelines (98/C 30/01), OJ No. C 030, 28.1.98, p. 1

[67] Francesca Bettio, Emilia Del Bono, Mark Smith,; "Employment and working time policies: A gender perspective", European Network of Experts on 'Gender and Employment, Report for the Equal Opportunities Unit, DG V, of the European Commission, July 1997

[68] Institute of Economics, University of Utrecht, "Overview of the state of the art studies: the labour market", Research Programme 1996/97

[69] Cardiff European Council, Presidency Conclusion of 15 and 16 June 1998, DOC/98/10

[70] Council Directive 97/80/EC of 15 December 1997 on the burden of proof in the cases of discrimination based on sex, OJ L14/6 of 10.1.98

[71] Council Directive (96/34/EC) of 3 June 1996 on the framework agreement on parental leave concluded by UNICE, CEEP and the ETUC, OJ No L 145, 19.6.96, p. 4

[72] see endnote 32 above

[73] Council Recommendation of 2 December 1996 on the balanced participation of women and men in the decision–making process (96/694/EC), No L 319, 10.12.96, p. 11

European Commission

Interim report on the implementation of the medium-term Community action programme on equal opportunities for men and women (1996 to 2000)

Luxembourg: Office for Official Publications of the European Communities

1999 — 34 pp. – 21 x 29.7 cm

ISBN 92-828-6999-7